high praise for pop propaganda

propaganda is as old as politics, and improving all the time. ever since the protections of the smith-mundt act were dissolved in 2012, americans have been recipients of a dazzling array of weaponized psychological research that used to be directed only at our enemies, and is now trying to control your mind.

fear not! for, in your hands, you hold a hip and handy compendium which identifies these techniques, and guides you back to sanity and logic.

kudos to dani katz for making this manual for right thought available at a time we need it most.

- robert forte
author + psychedelic scholar

pop
propaganda

an illustrated guide

written + illustrated
by
dani katz

duh.

for the critical thinkers,
the due diligencers and
those brave enough to dis-
mantle their worldviews +
cozy up to the question mark.

and the black sheep.

table of contents

<u>introduction</u>

our world is shaped by propaganda -
an umbrella term that describes
the deliberate + systematic efforts
to manipulate mass perceptions +
behaviors in service to the aim(s)
of the propagandist (also referred
to as social or cultural engineers).

propaganda is used to manufacture
consent for otherwise hidden, and
often nefarious aims. the practice
aims to deceive the public into
thinking our ideas, preferences,
allegiances + behaviors are being
generated organically, through our
own free will, when they are, in fact,
being engineered by those behind
the scenes, manipulating our culture to serve the agendas of the
few.

as propaganda is everywhere +
unrelenting, as well as - by nature -
covert - i have compiled this illustrated compendium of key phrases,
tools + tactics so as to shine a light
on the strategies being used to
(attempt to) manipulate us.

knowledge is power. when we clue
in to the techniques being used to
(attempt to) engineer our consent,
we are thus empowered to with-
draw said consent, and to come
together to co-create a new and
better world - one based on truth
and transparency, that serves the
greatest good of all.

pop propaganda

blarf
blarf
blarf
blarf
blarf
blarf
blarf

group think

propaganda is reliant upon group think. as the cultural engineer is tasked with manipulating the masses, she must eradicate the peskiness of individual thinking, or thinking at all.

hiya, group think!

group think refers to a phenomenon wherein the members of a group are coerced, or manipulated into conforming to a singular opinion, idea or perspective.

under the spell of group think, people's reasoning functions become impaired, which allows them to behave illogically, and irrationally.

group think is reliant upon the illusion of unanimity, which has the propagandist censoring conflicting ideas + opinions, and demonizing the opposition.

when under the spell of group think, followers are emboldened to break moral + ethical codes of conduct,

worst flooding in recorded history!

<u>half-truths + lies</u>

edward bernays, the godfather of propaganda, instructed would-be social engineers to tell <u>some</u> truth, but <u>never</u> the whole truth. successful propaganda relies on half-truths, manipulated, out-of-context truths, and flat-out lies to deceive the public into signing onto their agendas.

propaganda achieves its goals by any means necessary, and cares not a single whit for ethics or morality. to this end, those who push propaganda are in the habit of twisting facts, making stuff up, hiring crisis actors to pretend they're sick or wounded or traumatized, or "whistleblowers" to claim they were witnesses to crimes or ethical lapses.

the propagandist will write an article comprised of 99% factual information with the sole intention of pushing a single falsehood to manipulate an entire nation/planet.

BELIEVE US
magazine
Earth DEAD by Christmas.
Why It's All YOUR Fault

<u>fear</u>

social engineers use fear
to control the populace.
they do this by exagger-
ating the terrible stuff +
suppressing the wonderful
stuff.

worst case scenarios are
presented as absolute inev-
itables that will definitely,
for surely happen; and that
our only recourse is to be
very, very afraid, and to do
whatever the overlords in
charge tell us to do, to safe-
guard our "health", "safety"
and "freedom".

fear hormones shut down
our cognitive capacities +
make us easier to control
+ manipulate. that's why
our media and our medical
paradigm are lousy with
the stuff.

believe
this
buy
this
do this

the trusted leader

it's possible that trusted leaders were - at some point - honest humans occupying leadership positions. these days, trusted leaders are influencers, celebrities and billionaires. remember, people caught in the grips of group think don't actually think ; they follow. they follow trusted leaders.

trusted leaders don't need to have any real, personal connection to the propaganda they're swilling. it's not about the product, the movement or the op they're shilling, it's about their trusted leadership, and the magnetism it generates when it comes to herding the masses.

i would implement
changes to drug
policy, as violent
crime has skyrocketed
during your term.

you're a terrible
mother + you smell
bad.

ad hominem

the ad hominem is a strategy wherein - instead of ad-
dressing or challenging the
ideas someone espouses - the
propagandist (or the person
he is propping up) will attack their character, or some
unrelated behavior. indicative
of having zero proverbial legs
to stand on, ad hominems are
employed to deflect, distract
and dehumanize by attack-
ing a person, instead of con-
fronting the ideas or behavior
in question.

projecting ill intent is a com-
monly employed ad hominem
tactic, wherein the person doing the deflecting (aka: he who
is working with the cultural
engineer) alleges to be a psychic
mind reader, while claiming
the person whom he is ad hom-
ineming (yes, it's a verb) had
nefarious or unsavory inten-
tions.

"the lab leak..."

"...the lab leak."

repetition is the social engineers' a-#1, go-to tool. the strategy is simple: take the lie, the half-truth, the exagerration, the false equivalence or the slander, and repeat it over + over + over again, until the masses have bought into it - hook, line and sinker.

repetition is a clue that allows the truth-seeker to know where the propagandist is attempting to steer the populace. we don't need to know the details of the agenda at hand, or the false flag in the making; all we need to do is pay attention to the words + phrases the "trusted leaders" in the mainstream media space are repeating over + over again.

what happened:

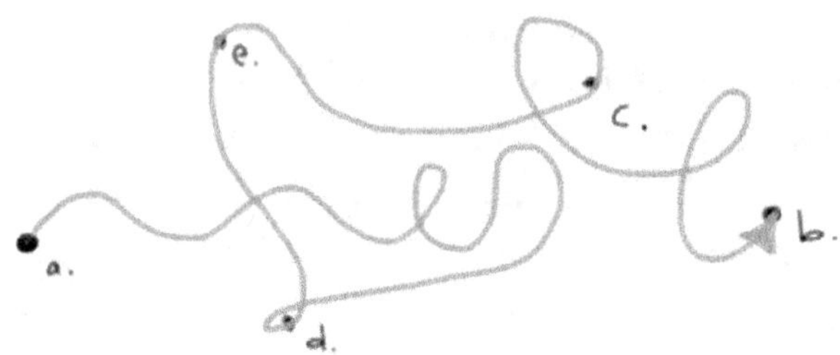

a. population
b. emissions
c. solar radiation
d. emfs
e. bpas

what they say happened:

a. good
b. republican

reductivism

propaganda is reliant upon extreme oversimplification. reductivism is the practice of reducing complex ideas into narrow, black or white iterations.

reductivism allows for no nuance or grey areas. it takes multi-layered situations + circumstances, and attempts to boil them down to shallow, oversimplified shell versions meant to obscure details + specifics that would invite deeper examinations + dialogues.

polarities such as good/bad, better/worse are used to reduce + oversimplify, as are false dichotomies, which attempt to whittle a variety of options down to only two.

i have some concerns
about the curriculum...

<u>doublespeak</u>

doublespeak uses deliber-
ately misleading language
to obscure facts, + down-
play atrocities. it does this
by employing easily digestible
language to cloud otherwise
horrific scenarios and circumstances, as in rebranding
lies as "alternative facts", or
describing civilians killed by
military drone strike as
"collateral damage".

doublespeak can also invert
the truth entirely, as in the
infamous slogan from george
orwell's "1984": "war is peace.
freedom is slavery. ignor-
ance is strength."

there is also the double-
speak we see when an elect-
ed leader dodges a clear,
direct question with a bunch
of nonsense words that com-
municate all of nothing - be it
a glittering generality, or a
non-sequitor.

straws are privilege

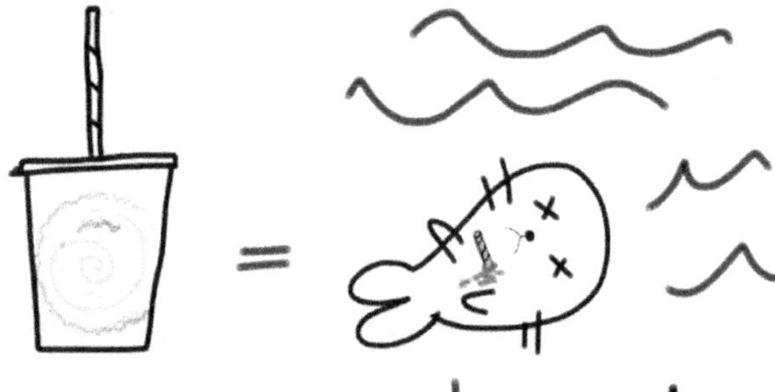

= and murder.

for every slurp,
a baby seal dies.

selfish people suck.

<u>emotional appeal</u>

the deliberate + constant manipulation of the human emotional state is the heart-beat of propaganda. it is the fundamental fuel that allows the social engineers to push their agendas forward.

their campaigns + shenanigans target our most primal, funda-mental emotions - grief, terror, love, pride, shame, hope, et al. fear of death, fear of loss, fear of loneliness, fear of survival - these big emotional triggers stimulate big emotional respon-ses that shut down the brain's logic centers. duly dumbed way down, the emotionally tipsy hu-man becomes an easy target for control.

when we are hopped up on cor-tisol, dopamine, serotonin or any of the myriad chemicals the body releases when emotionally activated, we more readily reach for the dangling carrots, empty promises + enslavement mechan-isms the cultural engineers are ever + always poised and ready to toss our way, disguised as they are as life rafts, because thank you, doublespeak.

mind control

the social engineers use mind control to persuade the masses to fall in line with consensus reality and all the ops and agendas that comprise it.

mind control techniques are vast + varied, often combining physical, as well as psycho-emotional abuse with brainwashing to fragment the minds of the victims, thus making them easier to control via compartmental-ized personalities.

technology + mass media are used as tools of mind con-trol, as subliminal messages are hidden (+ not so hidden) in images, symbols, song lyr-ics, storylines, dialogue and political + cultural theater, with the express purpose of indoctrinating the masses to fall in line with the control-lers' agendas.

MAGA
c.c.t.

---

egregious associations are a means of stereotyping the opposition. negative beliefs, allegiances + character traits are stapled to various ideas + behaviors in an attempt to bind them to the person they are meant to demonize.

egregious associations are repeated over + over + over again, thus creating an inextricable link between them + the people + groups to which they are being effectively stapled in the minds of the public.

egregious associations are also projected onto certain narratives or agendas to make them seem ridiculous or untrue. when the mainstream media started covering the "fake news" phenomenon, it was always accompanied by a "pizza-gate" graphic, thus linking the two ideas in the public mind, + creating an association between fake news and child trafficking/sexual abuse.

president + first lady

beautiful people

beautiful people are the backbone of modern propaganda. they can be rich, famous, genetically blessed, surgically enhanced or photoshopped just so. their souls can be wretchedly ugly, but when it comes to external appearance, or luxury lifestyles, culture deems them "beautiful".

proximity to the beautiful person garners social credit + status. the propagandists bank on this, and thus, utilize beautiful people to sell us on whatever they're shilling.

the social engineers' beautiful person is a key component in what the celtic mystics called "casting the glamor", wherein the public is enchanted, or put into a hynotic - and thus, highly suggestible - trance when presented with the shiny, sparkly allure of beauty, style, wealth + opulence.

100% of mice
tested experienced :
- blindness
- paralyses
- weight loss
- seizures
- death

"our new weight loss formula
has been proven 100%
effective in laboratory tests."
pharma
cabal

cherry-picking

cherry-picking is the practice of highlighting certain facts, while obscuring others, to persuade the audience to adopt a certain position or perspective. it is a type of half-truth, meant to manipulate the populace with only a few select pieces of the puzzle.

a politician might cherry-pick certain aspects of a proposed bill, while keeping a tight lip about other aspects; or a pharmaceutical company will publicize the wonders of a new drug, while failing to mention any adverse side effects, or the number of people who were injured during their clinical trials.

the media cherry-picks by taking quotes out of context, or editing videos in such a way as to force an angle or narrative that props up their agenda.

"teen heartthrob
mobbed by "white
supremacists!"

exaggeration

exaggeration is a hallmark of propaganda. because propaganda aims to manipulate people's emotions, those who utilize it employ exaggeration to really, really, really make their points land.

propagandists will oversell the good stuff, and harp all over the bad stuff, utilizing a hefty batch of adjectives and adverbs to manipulate the public's emotions, while getting their ideas across.

helped along by its cousin hyperbole, exaggeration is employed to make the good seem better, the bad seem worse, and to obscure any of the grey areas in between.

more dna from
the unwitting
student
volun-
teers

useful idiot

useful idiots are private
citizens who proselytize
for the forces that seek
to oppress them. having
been duly duped by propa-
ganda, useful idiots don't
fully understand the aims
of the folks or causes they
promote.

duly uninformed or mis-
informed, useful idiots
prop up people, groups,
organizations + movements
that do harm, and that
don't have their best in-
terests in mind.

useful idiots are a handy
tool for the social engineers,
as they loudly promote
the interests of those who
seek to enslave or take ad-
vantage of them, while
willingly doing the propagandist's bidding for them.

liberal republican

racist progressive

climate change denier

trumper

anti-v_xx_r

feminist libtard

transphobe karen

SJW

snowflake

conspiracy theorist

labeling + name-calling

hurling names at folks, and stapling them with labels is blood sport to the propagandist. labeling + name-calling are dehumanizing tactics that aim to put unique individuals in homogenized boxes, where they can be duly abused, stereotyped + marginalized.

while toddlers are taught not to call others names, the social engineers seem to be oblivious to this fundamental axiom of basic human decency + relational intelligence.

and so it is that the people are programmed to conflate behaviors with identity constructs, and to slap labels on folks who vote, think, believe + behave differently than they have been programmed to vote, think, believe + behave.

these labels + these names are themselves programmed with a host of negative connotations, egregious associations, and generalized "otherness" that generate feelings of ill-will and derision in those who are doing the labeling and the name-calling.

because of their dehumanizing nature, labels and name-calling are the gateway practices to violence and genocide.

demonization

propagandists go the dis-
tance to create the illusion
of unanimity amongst the
people they manipulate.
one of the ways they do
this is to demonize the opposition.

propagandists don't agree
to disagree. they agree to
make those who disagree
look like deranged psycho-
paths, and to turn their adherents against the disagre-
ers.

angles + strategies vary,
but the basic gist is to
shred the characters +
destroy the reputations
of anyone who opposes
their agenda.

unity
hope
we're all in this together.
for a better tomorrow
it's so inspiring!

glittering generalities

glittering generalities are vague words + phrases used to generate feel-good emotions, while communicating little to nothing at all.

often utilized in the realms of politics + advertising, glittering generalities use buzzwords like "change", "freedom", "unity", "equity", "family" + "prosperity" to generate positive feelings and associations.

slogans like "change we can believe in" or "for a better future" evoke hopeful feels, while offering nothing in terms of implementable action steps for the vision they are really only hinting at.

glittering generalities amount to fluffy filler statements comprised of otherwise empty words that sound good. they are the equivalent to going on a date with someone who's really good looking, but doesn't have much going on as far as depth or intelligence, and thus, has nothing interesting to say.

1. stage multiple mass shootings

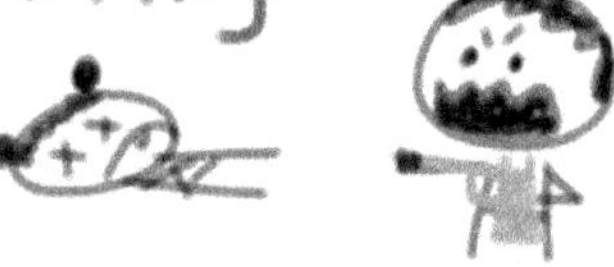

2. fan the flames of public outrage

3. "give in" to demands for gun control/disarmament

hegelian dialectic

sometimes referred to as "thesis-antithesis-synthesis" or "problem-reaction-solution", friedrich hegel devised this thinking strategy as a means of controlling political outcomes, as well as the psychology of the masses.

the hegelian dialectic starts off with an agenda that the social engineers want to implement. but, because the agenda doesn't serve the best interests of the masses, they disguise the agenda as the "solution" to a "problem" that doesn't exist... yet. and so it is that the propagandists go about crafting a "problem" (i.e. false flag) intended to generate a specific "reaction" from the public. the "reaction" then inspires (read: manipulates) the public to demand the very "solution" the nefarious overlords wanted to implement in the first place.

white privilege
toxic masculinity

<u>divide + rule</u>

also known as "divide and conquer", this strategy aims to counter the fact that a unified populace is impossible to control. and so it is that the social engineers go the distance to keep the collective polarized, + fighting amongst themselves, while blaming each other for the ills for which the ruling class (whom the propagandist serves) is actually responsible. duly divided, the people are easy to manipulate + control.

to this end, identity politics is an extremely useful strategy, as it pits various identitarian groups against one another, using incendiary talk of privilege + victimhood to polarize the people, + distract them with in-fighting, while the rulers occupy themselves with the task of making the world worse.

the two-party system is a prime example of divide + rule in full effect, to no one's benefit, save the puppet masters, who - surprise, surprise - actually control both parties.

new york times | spotify

fox | the atlantic | yahoo | cnn

reuters | vice | wired | slate | f x

espn | pbs | npr | facebook

washington post | msnbc | ap

youtube | politico | rolling stone

los angeles times | time | GQ | abc

usa today | forbes | google | nbc

cbs | sky | cbs | twitter | vogue

vanity fair | hbo | netflix

guardian | wikipedia | disney

tmz | mtv | showtime | viacom

cartoon network | instagram

discovery channel | hulu | BET

syfy | cnbc | usa | nickelodeon

simon + schuster | tbs | touchstone

mainstream media

also referred to as corporate media, or msm, the mainstream media is the propagandists' primary control mechanism/dissemination arm.

the phrase references the super very controlled media outlets owned by one of the 6 corporations that run them as allegedly separate entities. this includes radio, television, magazines, film, books, newspapers and digital media.

while shows, platforms + websites might - on the surface - appear to be independent, a closer examination will reveal a larger corporate parent company/overlord, censoring certain content, while force-feeding the approved narratives, along with heavy-handed servings of steaming hot propaganda served on a 24/7 blitz loop.

mainstream media doesn't create + distribute content just to serve their own interests of profit + control, but also to serve the interests of their advertisers, which -coincidentally- are also profit and control.

<u>false flag</u>

a false flag is an at-
tack or crisis staged by
one party with the express
purpose of placing the
blame on an entirely dif-
ferent party.

false flags are used to
justify "retaliatory" at-
tacks, or as an excuse to
impose certain restrict-
ions on the public, in service to their "freedom",
"health" and/or "safety".

false flags are generally
enacted by governments
or intelligence agencies
who obscure the fact that
they were the responsible
parties, while leaping to
blame completely different
parties for the events, so
they can attack, invade
or seize their people's
property and/or liberties.

9/11 was an inside job
the c.i.a. killed jfk
tin foil
khazaria! tartaria!
Satanic reptilians run the world.
the moon is fake

the crazy conspiracy theorist

demonizing the opposition is a classic propaganda strategy. one of the ways the social engineers do this is to make it seem like the truth-teller is a nut-job, and to brush off her ideas as "conspiracy theories".

the phrase "conspiracy theory" was co-opted by the c.i.a. in the 1960s as a way to shut-down intelligent discourse + dissuade people from digging into their own research. the term is now used to discount information that runs counter to mainstream narratives + agendas, as well as those who share it.

by the same token, insanity is consistently projected upon those who dare counter the propagandist's agenda. whether by gaslighting, cherry-picking or emotional manipulation, the idea that the truth-teller is crazy is put forth to discount the ideas he espouses, and to assassinate his character.

scapegoating

scapegoating is the act of blaming a person or group for something terrible they had nothing to do with, and then mistreating them as punishment for the act they didn't even commit. minority groups are historically used as scapegoats.

the strategy accomplishes two things: it allows the perpetrator(s) to evade responsibility for the atrocity in question, + it divides the populace.

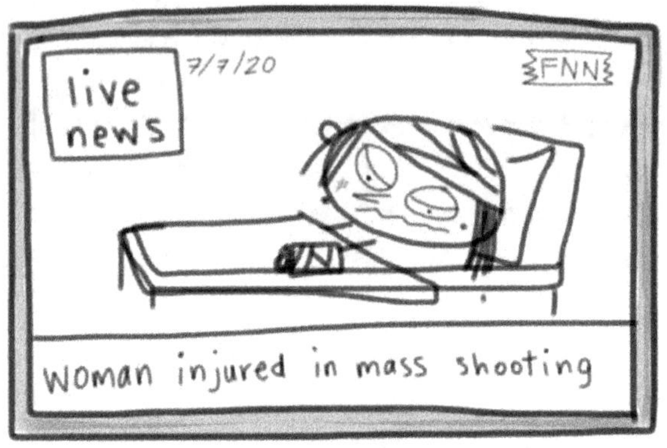

live news
7/7/20
FNN
Woman injured in mass shooting

live news
7/10/20
FNN
terrorist hostage speaks

crisis actor

crisis actors are hired theater-folk who are planted at various large-scale crisis events to play the roles of victims. these can include bombings, pandemics + mass shootings.

while their roles go largely uncredited, crisis actors are paid for their efforts with both currency and photo-ops, which are smeared all over the mainstream media, along with incendiary captions and hyperbolic headlines.

propagandists go to great lengths to make it seem like crisis actors are real-deal victims, despite the fact that many do double-duty on multiple false flags, raising many a "conspiracy theorist's" eyebrow.

meat
is
murder
bleeding heart
liberal

MAGA

e = mc²

dumb blonde

stereotyping

stereotyping is the practice of projecting rigid and reductive standards of behavior + characteristics upon a person or group. stereotyping seeks to homogenize otherwise unique individuals based on race, religion, gender, interest or allegiance.

stereotyping is used to marginalize certain groups, furthering the fragmentation and polarization in the social engineers' ongoing divide and rule efforts.

the practice denies our shared humanity, as well as the uniqueness of our individual paths + experiences, seeking to corral us into cages forged of bigotry + intolerance.

microchips
save lives.

bad actor

bad actors are inserted into the public sector where they pretend they are aligned against the agenda of the propagandist, when, in fact, they are acting on its behalf.

bad actors can be corporate shills, government folks, celebrities, "experts", scientists, doctors, media makers - you name it.

bad actors are sent into various organizations to make it seem like they are on board with the mission, when they are actually working against it.

wanna buy
some candy for
charity, mister?

no, thank you.

charity
hater.

(diabetic)

false dichotomy

a false dichotomy is a specific kind of reductive oversimplification in which two diametrically opposed points of view are presented as the only options, when other possibilities are available.

"either you are with us, or you are against us" is a classic example of a false dichotomy, as is "if you don't vote for me, you ain't black".

false dichotomies aim to fragment the world into two oppositional categories. the specific polarity constructs are irrelevant. the goal is to force a divide - to coerce people into choosing sides, and then injecting tension and ill-will between them.

kiki kramer: 1st grade twerk.
champion

demoralization

a subversive strategy, to be sure, demoralization is the practice of slowly eroding a society's values and standards by elevating morally + ethically questionable behavior through music, media, cultural movements and academic indoctornation (among oh-so-many other means).

demoralization is what has our culture sexualizing young children, cluttering the airwaves with songs about bling, blunts + broads, and elevating substance abuse, promiscuity, apathy and intolerance through media, entertainment, education + "journalism". duly demoralized, society erodes into chaos, making it harder and harder for the populace to motivate, thrive, unify and/or coordinate to course correct their culture and their world.

do you plan to
visit the orphans?
climate change
is patriarchy's
fault.

the red herring is a distraction tactic wherein the cultural engineer (or the minion doing her dirty work for her) presents information that has all of nothing to do with the topic at hand, to steer the conversation away from what is actually relevant.

oftentimes, the red herring constitutes a leap of illogic, as in a person stating: "bananas are racist," to which the social engineer responds: "bananas have potassium. we all know potassium is an equal opportunity mineral. potassium couldn't possibly be racist. now, borium on the other hand... borium has always been insensitive to issues of gender equality. in my new blue schpiel, i plan to eradicate this outdated myth of gender altogether, and relocate the species to mars."

disinformation agent

the disinformation agent is a master of disguise. he may come in the guise of your favorite podcast host, potty-mouthed comedian, or self-proclaimed independent journalist. she will speak valuable and refreshing truths, and even vocally oppose the dominant narratives that the propagandist is paid to prop up.

alas, while the disinformation agent speaks worthy truths 99% of the time, there is that lingering 1%, wherein she drops a hefty sprinkling of propaganda into the eyes + ears of her unwitting audience, who see her as a rebel truth-teller, as someone who stands against the establishment, + whom they can trust. this, of course, is false.

the disinformation agent (also called "controlled opposition") is working with the very agents he claims to oppose, and is deliberately misleading the public on their behalf.

bread + circuses

the expression "bread and circuses" was coined under the ancient roman empire. the phrase served as commentary on what passed for political leadership in the day, wherein the qualities of leadership, policy or even lifestyle were utterly irrelevant, as long as the people were kept fed + distracted with whatever passed as entertainment back then - be it chariot races, gladiator battles or throwing christians to the lions (the old school version of cancel culture).

the phrase is just as relevant today as it was back then, with folks choosing to "netflix 'n chill" while their children are indoctrinated, civil liberties seized + democracy shredded at an ever-quickening pace, in the name of safety, equity + social acceptance.

stay gray

indoctrination

indoctrination is the process
of repeating an ideology, belief
structure or means of thinking,
repeatedly and with feeling, such
that a person accepts it without
question.

most public schools operate as
indoctrination camps, wherein
students are not taught <u>how</u>
to think, rather they are told
<u>what</u> to think.

indoctrination allows for no
diversity of thought, instead
holding the adherents to a singular worldview or perspective,
while dissuading them from
thinking for themselves, outside
of the narrow confines to which
they have been trained to adhere.

the future
is female

My body,
my choice.
mask
up,
selfish!

<u>cognitive dissonance</u>

human beings tend to reject
paradox. the discomfort that
comes from holding two (or more)
opposing beliefs can be a hefty chal-
lenge to bear. the ensuing agita-
tion inspires us to seek out information that will resolve the
confusion.

this is where propaganda comes
in, smearing the controlled media
space with fear, lies + misinforma-
tion spewed by an endless slew of
trusted leaders + beautiful people
churning out the same fake narrative on a 24/7 multi-platform
blitz, drowning out any alternative
perspectives, which the controllers
have most likely censored, anyway.

duly programmed, people experi-
encing cognitive dissonance reject
new information that threatens
the validity of their programmed
beliefs, while taking many a leap of
illogic in rationalizing + doubling
down on beliefs + behaviors that
run counter to their innate sense
of right + wrong.

billionaire sobs as
he is convicted of crimes
against
humanity.

☐ fact   ☒ fake

the billionaire welled up,
and only a couple tears
let loose, so he did not
sob, because he
barely even cried.
this story is 100% fake.

fact-checkers

fact-checkers comprise ai alogrithms and untrained, unqualified folks who google stuff and then invert, evade, misconstrue + lie in service to the larger lie(s) being pushed by the propagandists.

utilized by the exact same entities that fund + certify them to "check" the illegitimate veracity of their fictitious narratives, as well as to "debunk" real-deal truth that might de-rail their nonsense, fact-checkers are both doublespeak + hegelian dialectic rolled into one ridiculous sham.

in reality, fact-checkers are tools of censorship that would be more appropriately called "fake narrative pushers".

X
A
x 1,000,000,000

op

op is shorthand for operation, meaning the specific
scheme the propagandist is
pushing.

there are multiple ops run-
ning at any given time; and
various propaganda projects
may be executed to serve
several ops at once.

an op can be small or massive-
be it to generate demand for
a new consumer product, or to
initiate a race war.

traditionally used to refer to
c.i.a. operations, such as operation paperclip, project mk
ultra + operation mockingbird,
the word is now employed to refer to the larger project behind
the propaganda campaign in
question - be it a military coup,
depopulation, or the deploy-
ment of a global surveillance
system.

information overload

though, often brushed off as a mere side effect of expo- nentially accelerating tech- nological advancement, in- formation overload is a delib- erate social engineering strat- egy meant to confuse + overwhelm the populace.

the idea is to inundate us with entertaiment, news (real + fake), gossip, screen captchas, os up- dates, user agreement changes, multiple-factor authorization codes, technological learning curves, et al, so that we are too frazzled, distracted and shell-shocked to take in the largesse of what is really go- ing on.

duly drowning in information overload, we have neither the bandwidth or capacity to question the direction in which the cultural engineers are at- tempting to steer us, struggling as we are to just keep up.

about the author

dani katz is a real-deal, bonafide journalist, despite the censor-ship, the deplatforming and the mainstream media's attempts to silence her. she received a masters degree in journalism from usc, and has since published hundreds of articles (alongside her chicken-scratchy line drawings) in los an-geles times, la weekly, vice, teen vogue + santa fe reporter, among oodles of others. she also served as lead writer/researcher on "plandemic indoctornation" - the most censored documentary in history, to date.

a quantum languaging consultant, coach + teacher, katz is the author of "word up: little languaging hacks for big change" + "yes, i am". she lives on a high desert hilltop where she teaches new earth badasses how to create + transform reality with their every word.